X

by
Xtina Marie

A HellBound Books LLC Publication
Copyright © 2025 by HellBound Books Publishing LLC
All Rights Reserved

Cover and art design by Luke Spooner
for
HellBound Books Publishing LLC

No part of this book may be reproduced, stored in a retrieval system, or transmitted by any means, electronic, mechanical, photocopying, recording or otherwise without written permission from the author
This book is a work of fiction. Names, characters, places and incidents are entirely fictitious or are used fictitiously and any resemblance to actual persons, living or dead, events or locales is purely coincidental.

www.hellboundbookspublishing.com

Poetry is nearer to vital truth than history. -Plato

Praise for Xtina Marie

"Poetry that jumps off the page and squeezes your heart. I loved every word." -*New York Times bestselling author, Alessandra Torre*

"Ever wanted to know what a person's soul looks like? In this vulnerable, eclectic book of poetry, the writer flays open her soul and bleeds onto each page, giving her readers a rare glimpse into the essence of who she is. Raw, beautiful, and poignant!" -*K Webster, USA Today Bestselling Author*

"Dark and delightful poet Xtina Marie has such a beautiful way with words—I'm a fan already, but 'Xtina's Greatest Hits' has me obsessed! I wanna make Xtina Marie wall collages and fill 100 notebooks in tiny black-print handwriting! Just kidding... mostly. (In all seriousness, read this book! It's dreamy.)" -*Staci Layne Wilson, author of the 'Rock & Roll Nightmares' book series*

"Xtina's poetry will transport you to the most tender part of your mind and heart. She will challenge you and reward you for spending time with her book." -*Debra Anastasia, USA Today bestselling novelist*

"Xtina Marie doesn't just have a way with words, she commands them. Her poems are heartbreaking, angry, poignant, and occasionally lethal. Which is exactly what poetry should be." -*Samantha Downing, USA Today bestselling author*

"A beautiful, raw, and moving tribute to the experience of being human. Do yourself a favour - stop what you're doing and immerse yourself in this most lovely book of poetry." -*Melanie Summers, award-winning, Amazon best-selling author of The After Wife*

dedication:

My 10th book of poetry is dedicated to my mom. She was one of my biggest supporters and always always told me what a great writer I was, even when I didn't believe it myself. She left me 8 years ago and I miss her every day. Hopefully one of these years I'll complete that novel she always wanted me to write.

acknowledgements:

Firstly, a big thank you to James Longmore. Without him Dark Musings would have been a distant memory, stuck in no man's land with that crappy 1st publisher we don't speak of anymore. Now look at us! Hundreds of amazing HellBound Books, horror cons under our belts and even company t-shirts now!

Shout out, as always to Luke Spooner, my wonderful cover artist! I say *this is what I want,* and he says, *I got you!*

A big thank you to Denise Jury for catching my typos and boo boos after all these years!

An honorable mention goes out to my kids, Hali and Shawn. Hopefully one of them will make sure to place me in a nice nursing home when I'm old.

And last, but definitely not least, thank you, Christian. The dark poems might come fewer and far between now, but you give me a safe space to exorcise my old demons!

contents:

Wildfire
With Scarred and Damaged Arms
Cruel, Grey Skies and Indifference
Thank You
Above All
I'm Sinking
Hints of Summer
Once More, Anchored
A Flimsy Thing
Cherry-Flavored Icees, Anticipation and First Love
A Burning House
Cowering in the Chaos
Even in the Summer Heat
My Soundtrack
We Were Here
The Edge
Good Girl
Restlessness
Wilted
Lost in You
Jagged Scars & Naked Hearts
Inspiration
Sunday Dinner
Blissfully High
A Roaring Fire
Satan's Kisses
His Favorite Song
Simple Things We Take for Granted
Repairs
Something Else
Something Wicked

Hidden Scars
…and I Shiver
Utter Depression
Endless Florida Heat
As a Child
January's Lies
Distance and Scattered Months
Background Noise
Searching for the Shadows
The Chasm Spread
Like a Heartbeat
Artistic Straitjacket
The Closest We Will Ever Come
The Cyber Poet
Pretty Sins
Hidden in the Chaos
Slowly Becoming a Roar
Pure Hearts
Toxic Self-Righteousness
Summer Vacations
Keep Your Beaches
2024
Feral Animals
Intricate Blue Ribbons
The Crescendo
Moonlit Memories
A Winter Night
Who I Was
Stoned
A Chilly March Morning
The Hook
Frigid
Dancing in the Breeze
Duck Duck Goose
Ghostly Lore & Thick Southern Accents

(My Yearly Summer Poem)
Blank Pages
Soul Mates
Love isn't Enough
Black Eyes
Separate Ways
The Rents
Marley
Compromise
Alive
My Demons
Oddly Eternal
Widowmaker
Tuesday
A Little Lost

About the Author

Wildfire

she's like
a wildfire
all hot and chaotic
and burning
everything
in her wake
despite
heroic efforts
to thwart
the destruction

no one can tame
disaster

With Scarred and Damaged Arms

The scars
decorating
her arms
are proof
she's still here
another day

despite
the mental
torment
constantly
plaguing her

whispering to her
she'll never
be good enough

never make a
difference

never amount to
anything

she no longer
believes
differently

it's her truth
and she's tired
of fighting
the overpowering
oppressive
thoughts
that scream
her insecurities

they know her
they love her
they embrace her

with scarred
and damaged arms

*you will
always
be my
white picket fence*

Cruel, Grey Skies and Indifference

I often feel
like a wildflower
in winter
trying so hard
to maintain
my vivid
color
and joyous
disposition
while everything
around me
begins to decay
and wither

yet still
I continue
to look up
hopefully,
toward where
the sun once shone
and the warmth
nourished me
with its
vibrance

but I'm met
with cruel, grey skies

Xtina Marie

and indifference

sometimes
it's almost
too much

to bear

Thank You
For Christian

To all the
non bio-dads
out there
on Father's day
working harder
than they
should have to
because
some men
might be fathers
but will never
be dads…

thank you

thank you for
loving
a child
that you
didn't create
and for healing
a hurt
you didn't
inflict

thank you

thank you
for stepping up
when others
made the choice
to step down
and for having
to be the bad guy
at times
to ensure
you impart
all of the wisdom
you've gained
in your years

thank you

thank you for
the true meaning
of unconditional love
and support
and all the
things
that *should*
come
with being
a dad
but unfortunately
sometimes
does not

thank you

Above All

laughter
and
good experiences
touch
the heart

above all
be full of
love

I'm Sinking

A melancholic
sadness
lives
inside me

a deep
fear
I'll always
have

lost
in my own
creation

I'm sinking

Xtina Marie

*I've been
scattering ashes
in my head*

Hints of Summer

Hints of Summer
fall from
the sky
in lazy
warm drops
like salty tears
tracking down
faces of
toddlers
crying
because their
bottle
was a few
minutes late
and I mourn
with them
on this longest day
as we gather
to say goodbye
to cool evenings
and the hopeful
renewing
of Spring
while looking
toward
sweltering nights
and the visiting

Xtina Marie

fireflies

Once More, Anchored

The exhaustion
that comes
after a sound
beating
is what I
crave

everything
quiets
stills
calms
inside of me
and my brain
resets
with each lash
of the crop

with every swing
of the paddle
I can breathe,
the world comes
back into focus,
and I am
once more,
anchored

A Flimsy Thing

I've been trying
for weeks
to make
peace
but there
is no hiding

Summer
is a
question mark,
a flimsy thing
but still
here

Cherry-Flavored Icees, Anticipation and First Love

I was a teen
in the 80s
when lazy summers
were spent
watching the
flash of fireflies
out at the basketball hoop
with our boom box
blaring Madonna and
Janet Jackson,
hearts full of
cherry-flavored icees
anticipation and
first love

we had big hair
long earrings
attitude and
so much time
to do
absolutely nothing
but live hard
everyday
in the heat,
drinking from
a neighbor's
garden hose

coming home
when we were
hungry or
the streetlights
came on

we rolled our eyes
at authority because
we knew it all,
no one understood us
and most of the time
we were raising
ourselves
even though
our parents
were only doing
the best that
they could

sometimes I long
to go back
to when things
were simpler,
before careers
and kids
and car payments
but then
True Blue
comes on
the radio

and my heart
is again full of
cherry-flavored icees
anticipation and
first love

*the spark
burned
out*

*killed by
his wordage*

A Burning House

I used to
live in a
burning house,
watching
the fire
crawl up the
curtains
with every
bitter,
vile word
you spoke

each breath
I took
labored and
painful as I
inhaled the smoke
and lies
you served
daily with your
morning coffee,
a smile on your
deceitful lips
as you passed
the sugar bowl
laced with poison

Xtina Marie

I turned
a blind eye
as my skin blistered…
as it bubbled
and blackened,
the acrid smell
hanging horribly
in the air
after each
long night
alone in a
bed for two

I ignored
the appendages
that turned
to ash,
falling soundlessly
to the ground
until I tried
to escape
but there was
no longer
legs in which
to escape with
just a pile
of smoldering remains

The flames
consumed

𝒳

and yet
I sat next
to you
while we ate
our dinner
in the
deafening
solitude
together
but alone
and I

watched

as we burned

Cowering in the Chaos

you were a
a beach house
in a hurricane--
all pretty
decorations
and sharp edges…
as long as
I kept
the candles
stocked
and battened
down the
hatches,
I'd be safe
from the
impending
storm

but I
was never
that prepared,
and cowered
in the chaos
—powerless—
the only
sounds audible
were the howling

X

of the wind
and the steady
drum of rain
as they
beat upon
the walls with
undisguised rage
and fury

every storm
I'd tell myself
this time
I'd be ready
this time
will be
different
this time
I'd be equipped…

until
I was again

cowering
in the chaos

that   was   you

Xtina Marie

*you're my
favorite
love letter*

Even in the Summer Heat

We used to
whisper
late at night,

legs tangled
together
even in the
summer heat

laughing in
hushed voices
at things
that seemed

funny
at the time

years later

you only
talked to me
if you had a
complaint
or something
for me to do

and all the
laughter

you seem to
have saved up
for your
co-worker

the cute
little number
whose ass
filled out her jeans
way better than mine

and the only whispers
were still
late at night

but came from
the porch
while you talked
on the phone
until the sun
came up

even in the
summer heat

My Soundtrack

I want to write
beautiful poetry
on a rooftop,
the sounds of
the street below
my soundtrack

I want to
people watch
with the birds
and share
my verse
so that they too
can sing along

We Were Here

Let's hop in
the car
without
packing,
no destination
in mind--
just drive
until we
find some
cheap motel
with
questionable
art on the
wall
and a
dried-up pool
out back…
we'll kiss
and touch
and fuck
on the scratchy
bedspread
before falling
asleep
in each other's
arms…
we'll wake

before the sun
and eat stale
Fritos
from the
vending machine
for breakfast
after scrawling
a note on
the bathroom mirror
that says
we were here

The Edge

sometimes
the road
twists and turns
and you
never can tell
just how close
you are
to the edge

Good Girl

Occasionally
I need to be
reminded
of my place—
of my role

with deep
red marks
across my ass
from the
cane, or crop
or paddle

with pain
and discomfort
as I lower
myself gingerly
on colorful bruises
into a chair

with tears falling
from swollen eyes,
a hoarse throat

from crying out
and muscles weak
from tensing in

Xtina Marie

anticipation
of the next blow

I'm reminded
of my place—
my role

when you
brush the hair
from my
sweaty neck,
and whisper
softly…

Good girl

Restlessness

restlessness
agitated me

    sometimes
        my imagination
        created fire

and desire

be satisfied
with
        tranquility

Xtina Marie

Wilted

There's a poem
in the wilted roses
but I just can't
bring myself
to write it

Lost in You

drunk...
I blame
you

remember
when you
made me
believe
I knew you?

the slow dance
at 2a.m.
the long talks
that lasted til
the sun came up
laying on blankets
in the backyard,
your eyes
that followed me
through the house
smoldering and
lighting me
on fire

writing this
—hungover—
I'm finally

Xtina Marie

forgetting
to be
lost in you

Hazy Contentment

Sometimes,
I visit you
in my memories;
recalling
warm summer
evenings
on the weekends
and scrabble
on the floor
of your
little studio
apartment,
a slight breeze
from the open
screen door
disturbing
my hair…
the smoke
from your cigar
billowing softly
around me,
swirling in the
light spilling
in from the
setting sun
and I'm not
quite sure

Xtina Marie

if it's the
late August heat
or the memory
of you
that warms me with
hazy contentment

Jagged Scars & Naked Hearts

shhh…

kissing
and touching
and fucking

loud and imperfect
on messy, slick sheets

leaving jagged scars
on exposed skin
and naked hearts

Inspiration
For: Ro

She says
she's not a
mannequin

and she's not

she's yellow
and sunshine
and flowers in
her hair

she's a rose
and fluttering
eyelashes
and pirouettes
in the
summer rain

she's a sticky
red lollipop
and a radiant smile
with a flirty sundress
in the Boston
winter

she's a tattered

and used copy of
Emily Dickenson's
greatest works
every page dogeared

she's a broken heart
in love
with being
in love

and she'll always be
my biggest
inspiration

Sunday Dinner

Father was
around
too much,
and we all
knew why…

Sunday dinner
forced discomfort
and sobriety and
a tiny act of
rebellion

it was worth it

Blissfully High

It's wishing
and kissing
and fire...
so blissfully high,
adrift with
rushing desire

A Roaring Fire

Certainly,
there was no
mistake
a fire was
beginning
a roaring fire
close enough
for warmth
yet far enough
away to escape
being burned

Satan's Kisses

waltzing
inside a
dead girl's eyes,
I was bewitched
by her blackness

her dreams were
quite insane—

all fire and
thunder
and Satan's
kisses

I think
it was
love

His Favorite Song

Long Cool Woman
was his favorite song
but I wasn't
cool and I
definitely
wasn't long,
—barely reaching 5'—
and maybe
that's why
he always liked
to remind me
I'd never have it all

Simple Things We Take for Granted

I write about
the trips we take
to Kentucky
and the haunted inn
we stayed at
even though
I never saw
a ghost there,
or the times
we head to
North Carolina
and the scenic
drive through
the mountains
where we lose
cell signal
for most of the way

I write about
the amazing
holidays
with you
and our yearly
hippie costumes
on Halloween,
waking up
with the sun

to cook
the turkey
for Thanksgiving
and spending
December
dreaming of
a white Christmas

but I seldom write
about this:

lazy weekends
lying around
the house
watching trash tv
in our underwear,
playing board games
while listening to
80s hair bands
and eating snacks
we bought
for date night

the simple things
we sometimes
take for granted

the things
we will miss
should we

stop making time

to do them

Repairs

Try as I might
I could never
fix
what you
broke

and I stopped
trying
when I realized
it was
never mine
to repair

Something Else

When I can't sleep
I think about
everything
and a lot
of nothing

…maybe that
silly moment on
Friends and how
Susan wasn't
really a
bad person,
just misunderstood

…and that I
don't know how
I am going to
deal with
losing Charlie;
or if I'll know
when it's time
to say goodbye

…and next time
I make
unstuffed
cabbage rolls

for dinner
I definitely
need to
add more
red pepper

…or how
I don't miss
a thing
about him
but I still
feel something
when he
crosses
my mind

…and how
we never know
when the current
chapter ends
until we are
halfway through
the next one,
and shouldn't there
be some warning?

…and that I pray
for a meteor
to take us
all out at once

so I never have
to know
life without you
because I
honestly
do not think
I could go on

…and that
I'll definitely
stop eating
granola parfaits
so late at night…
if it was even
that parfait,
I suppose
it could have been
something else

Something Wicked

The first hints
of fall
waltz in
with a
nonchalant
September breeze
and a
scattering of
dead and dying
leaves dancing
to the ground

something wicked
whispers
between
the rustling
of the foliage
and the
warm breath
from a lover's
carnal thoughts
tickling my cheek

I can taste
caramel apple
and excitement
on his tongue

as I light
a candle
and watch
its flickering
flames
twirl in
the night air

Hidden Scars

night terrors
come to visit
occasionally…
a mess
that refuses
to hide the scars

.and I Shiver

I watch you
from the
reflection
of the mirror,
following your
movements
and tracing
every line
of your face
with my eyes

because—

it's you
but it's
horrifyingly

not you

a deep fake
a fraud
a cruel imitation
of the person
I know so well,
the person
I love

and I am filled
with equal parts
fear and
excitement

maybe
I am seeing
the hidden parts
of you,
the things that
you hope
no one ever
finds out…
and what if I
find things that
can help me
understand you
better?

but what if

what if
I am seeing
some evil
doppelganger,
a clone,
an imposter
that hides
in your
reflection

and wishes to
crossover
to this world
if given the
opportunity

I lie next to you
in bed at night
and wonder
about that scar –
the one high
on your left shoulder,
the one that
I could swear
used to be
on your right

...and I shiver

Utter Depression

A dark day in autumn…
melancholy shades of evening
gloom poetically terrible
from bleak vacant trees
blossoming with
utter depression,
a hideous sensation,
an icy, sinking dreariness
unnerving me

Endless Florida Heat

we fucked
and smoked
and drank warm beer
in the summer sun,
oppressive and heavy
everyday,
much like that arm
you slung around
my shoulders
when you were too
tipsy to walk
on your own

I fought with
your demons
more than I
fought with you
because the you
I knew
was not you
anymore
but some stranger
that sometimes still
wore your smile

I can't recall exactly
when the novelty

Xtina Marie

of you
wore off
but it was somewhere
around the 6th beer,
our life on repeat
everyday
in the endless Florida heat
and your arm
oppressive and heavy
around shoulders
that had grown tired
of holding you up

As a Child

I wish that
I could
s t o p
the hourglass
on some snowy evening
in December
as we are
watching icy
white flakes fall
lazily from the sky
and we sit
by the lights
of the Christmas tree,
your eyes reflecting
the magic I feel
in the air,
the anticipation
filling me with
the same joy
I felt as a child

January's Lies

January's lies
bathe us in
the deceit of
warmth
while we watch
from frosted
windows,
sipping hot cocoa
or coffee,
our fluffy colored socks
artificially cheerful
on the frigid hardwood

Distance and Scattered Months

spiraling past muted flowers
I kiss goodbye
empty evenings
filled with distance and
scattered months

unnoticed

Background Noise

I don't
have the
time
anymore

too busy

pictures
will become
just stories
when
you're not
alive anymore

I don't need
to know
the meaning
of that song
you used to play
on repeat
anymore

it's just background noise

sometimes
my muse
is silent
even though
the silence
is deafening

Searching for the Shadows

Each year, I find
I write about
the changing seasons
and the electricity
I can feel
in the air
as the flowers
awaken and start
stretching their faces
to the warming sun
and I wonder
why it is that
instead of reveling
in the warmth,
using it to heal and heat
aging bones,
I bow my head
and search for the shadows
looking for the weeds
that continue to
grow even in
the dead of winter

I Feel the Chasm Spread

I remember when
I was her world,
when she'd cling
to my hand
if we were
at the grocery store
or out running
an errand…
when she'd babble
nonstop about
anything that
came to mind,
entertaining me
for hours
with her curiosity…

I am not sure
when I stopped being
the person she called
in an emergency
or who she went to
for advice
about her love life,
but I feel the
chasm spread
everyday
as my phone calls

Xtina Marie

go to voicemail
and my texts
stay unread

I suppose
I've done my job
successfully
when I've
taught my children

    to stop
        needing me

Like a Heartbeat

we may laugh
at times
but the hurt
rises on the wind
and the pain
is endless;
like a heartbeat

Artistic Straitjacket

I have this
artistic straitjacket
I buckle
around me
every so often

it's tight—
cutting off
the circulation
between
heart and mind

it suffocates
and binds
the words
scratching at my throat
begging to be
set free

so I swallow
them down
choking on
the bitter taste
of words
unspoken

The Closest We Will Ever Come

when I wake
the bed is cold

bad dreams
light the bedroom

in sleep
as lovely as
the ugliest
flower

the closest
we will ever come
to love

The Cyber Poet

I'm sure he's
somewhere
between
heaven and hell
with a
cigarette
in one hand
and a pen
in the other,
cup of coffee
close by
just as steamy
as the poetry
he's still
creating

rip Bill

Pretty Sins

a doll
with dark thoughts,
my sins
were pretty
and took
what they wanted,
what I needed

Our rendezvous
is a farce
never resulting
in anything

Hidden in the Chaos

blank pages
stare back
at me
accusingly
wondering
where I have been
and I…

I am not sure

life
gets in
the way
sometimes

is the excuse
I give,
but it's
not the truth

the truth
is somewhere
else,
hidden
in the chaos
of work and laundry
and making the bed

and planning
dinner…

the truth
is in the final episode
of a show
I've been watching
or in the
last fifty pages
of the book
I am reading

distractions…
but from time to time

I need
to be distracted

from the chaos

*Somedays
I catch a glimpse
of the boy
you used to be*

Slowly Becoming a Roar

On nights the demons
in your head were loudest,
I began to hear
them too

death death death

starting with a whisper
and slowly becoming
a roar—
almost like
background noise
of a fan left on low
for too long—

blood blood blood

the smell of your
Black & Mild
swirling sweetly
around me,
I watch you down
the next beer,
wondering just
how many drinks it will take
to drown out the voices
so I can sleep

I clench my hands
at my sides
pretending not to
feel the sticky warmth of your
blood between my fingers

perhaps this is the night

I finally
let your demons
                                    win

Xtina Marie

Pure Hearts

upon summer's
thoughts
remain
cozy
lingering words
floating on the
sweet silence
of pure hearts

Toxic Self-Righteousness

ugliness
bathes the world
in its putrid
cesspool,
slowly washing
over humanity
in vile little doses
of bitterness and toxic
self-righteousness

Summer Vacations

together
we sprinted
toward
excitement
eventually
collapsing
on our backs
in the sand

Keep Your Beaches

Keep your
overcrowded beaches
with sandy shores
and oppressive heat,
the loud sun
blinding everything
in a harsh
blaze of fire

give me the
quiet rolling
Tennessee hills,
the warm breeze
dancing over
vibrant green fields,
honeysuckle
drifting lazily
on the air

sigh

2024

If this year
was a poem
all the stanzas
would only be
partially done

Feral Animals

We all think
we are good,
we are honest
we are noble
and kind

but underneath
all the layers
we keep
hidden
and buried
far below
the surface

we are nothing more
than feral animals
muffling our
guttural roars

Intricate Blue Ribbons

there are times
late at night,
while I am lying
in bed
that I hear
the sound of the
wallpaper peeling--
small sections
of pale yellow
surrounding
intricate blue ribbons
flaking off
to collect in a pile
on the dusty floor

but when I check
the next morning
I am always
shocked
to see the baseboards
clean, void of anything
but the dirt
gathering in
the corners

only then

X

do I remember

my walls

have never had

wallpaper

Xtina Marie

The Crescendo

reach
for the
crescendo,
every movement
a symphony of
determination
twirling to the
music of release,
the flourishing swells
pirouetting
with tears and sweat
til we're nothing
more than
arms, and limbs
and hearts and hands

Moonlit Memories

complete darkness--
guilt and remorse
embrace
innocent hearts…
together
we search for
a lifetime
beneath
moonlit memories

A Winter Night

darkly,
through the
thin frost of
empty rooms,
his eyes
remembered
the creaking loss…

the sounds
of familiar,
common things
were now
quiet

and the
broken sun
still slept

thus does
a winter night

Who I Was

someday
decades from now
one of my
great great grandkids
will stumble upon
my social media page
from some
long abandoned
platform
--is Myspace still around?--
and scroll past
hundreds of random
thoughts and activities
I shared,
clicking on videos posted
that I'd deemed
so interesting
at the time

or find
an old photo album
--because I'm old enough
to have been alive
when photo albums
were still relevant—
and thumb through

the pages,
getting a glimpse
of the life
I lived
and the things
that were
important to me

on that someday
I hope
they have fun
getting to know
who I
was

Stoned

no one's home
stoned
alone
out of my
mind
his eyes
those warm
brown eyes
I'm drowning
in the memory
of those eyes

A Chilly March Morning

if this is
the last poem
I write

let it be

the warmth
of the sun
shining through
clouds
on a chilly
March morning

The Hook

he was like
the most beautiful song
I'd ever heard;
the song I'd listen to
on repeat
on lonely nights
because the cadence
spoke volumes
to my
damaged soul

and in the darkness
the hook was
contagious,
even though
the lyrics
were a little too
muffled
to make out clearly

so I'd just
hum to the beat,
pretending
I understood
every soulful word
verse after verse

Xtina Marie

until we again
came to
the hook

but when the
music stopped

I realized

neither
one of us

knew

what the song
was about

Frigid

I'd curl around
your body
and stay there
til the last breath
seeped out
and the space
around us
turned

frigid

Xtina Marie

Dancing in the Breeze

Wandering
o'er hills,
golden daffodils
dancing in the
breeze

Duck Duck Goose

oh to be young
and naïve
and blissfully unaware
of the all of the
hardships, tragedies,
tears and heartaches
that life scatters about
aimlessly, it seems
as we age
almost as if tossing out
BINGO or lottery numbers

YOU get a raise!
YOU get an unexpected death!
YOU get a funky addiction!
YOU get a cool talent!

it's a terrifying game
of *duck duck goose*
but instead of
your friend
tapping your head lightly,
life sucker punches you
when your eyes
are closed
and before you've
successfully

Xtina Marie

caught your breath
from the last blow
another one is hurled
your way

Ghostly Lore & Thick Southern Accents

my heart belongs
to Tennessee
but Kentucky
whispers
to my soul
with the
hushed rustle
of the grass
as we speed down
backroads in the
summer,
hair stinging
my face and the
overhead sun
heating my skin

Tennessee is
Home Sweet Home
by the *Crüe* while *Kentucky* is
Sweet Home Alabama
by *Skynyrd* blaring from the radio
as the heady scent
of honeysuckle
lazily drips
from the trees
enticing me with

Xtina Marie

ghostly lore and thick
southern accents

I'll lay my head
in Tennessee
and hold
the Kentucky nights
close to my heart

like a past lover
I'll never quite
get over

(My Yearly Summer Poem)

summer
smells like
hotdogs on the grill
and roller skates,
badminton in the
back yard
and red kool-aid
while sweating
in the mid-day sun
listening to
Fight for Your Right to Party
on repeat

summer
smells like
frilly dresses
baring scraped knees
and musty church pews,
The old Rugged Cross
sung somberly
and off key
with Miss Teresa
at the piano
while we head
to the potluck

summer
smells like
Monday night football,
butterflies and first love,
whispers and giggles while
sneaking out the back door
and clumsy kisses
in the bed of
pickup trucks
as *I'm All Out of Love*
plays softly from the dash
on the radio

summer
smells like

freedom

Blank Pages

You were
a book I found
on the best-seller list
with the
eye-catching cover
and exciting synopsis,
the one I spent
good money on
and couldn't wait
to get home
to crack it open
and get lost
in the story

but all
your pages

were blank

Soul Mates

we lay in the sand
sweat beading,
rolling down
bodies golden
from the sweltering
Florida heat,
a little chilled
when the breeze
rolled over the water
and tousled our hair

we talked
about traveling the world,
if Bigfoot was real
and the meaning of life
while laughing
and nudging each other
playfully
with a familiarity
we claimed to have never
experienced before
as the sun dipped low
and moonbeams
cast shadows
in the sand

we passed a bottle
of cheap raspberry wine
back and forth
and confessed secrets
to one another,
things we'd never told
another human,
spoke of how
we must have known
each other in a former life
and that we were
soul mates
as the sun began
to dance over the waves,
gloriously majestic
in her brilliance

and as we made our way
through the sand
and to the parking lot
littered with
empty beer bottles
and crumpled up
fast food wrappers
we kissed sloppily,
tasting the stale wine
on each other's tongue
and promised
to get together real soon

Xtina Marie

but as I washed the sand
out of my hair
that evening
I realized
I had never asked him
his name

Love isn't Enough

when he's drunk
he likes to remind me
that he still
loves me,
and truth be told
I'm pretty sure
a part of me
will always
love him too

and then I remember
the benders—
the alcohol
that flowed steadily
like water
until the blackouts,
and paramedics rushing about
leaving mud on the
cheap government housing carpet
that I'd spend days cleaning
after a night of
IV drips and
beeping monitors

and the shouting—
almost nightly

spit flying and ugly words
hurling my way
like tiny knives
spraying hatred
like blood spurting
from my arteries,
and tears coating
glassy cheeks,
the sweet smell
of beer fermenting,
oozing from sickening pores
and neighbors
lowering their gazes
the next day
in apartment hallways
with feigned embarrassment
disguised as concern

so when he's drunk,
I like to remind him
that sometimes
love isn't enough

Black Eyes

unearthly cries
interrupted the night,
and the rain hid
the sadness
dripping from
black eyes
unwilling to say
goodbye

Separate Ways

amongst the chaos,
piped-in
carousel music
and sugary sweet scent
of funnel cakes
wafting on the
late summer breeze,
we walked and talked,
my hip innocently
bumping into yours
every few steps,
your soft chocolate eyes
crinkling at the corners
as you laughed
at something i said

i was sure it was love

and as we rolled around
on the dirty carnival grounds
behind the tilt-a-whirl,
my skirt hiked up to my waist,
i experienced my first love,
my first lust
and my first heartbreak
all in one night

under a starless sky
and the muffled radio playing
Journey's Separate Ways
from tinny speakers

The Rents

it was the early 90s
and grunge was
hitting the scene…
for some reason
our music
was a little more
depressing
than the fun and flirty
80s vibe
and we were
there for it,
screaming *Teen Spirit*
into our curling irons
while rolling our eyes
at the rents

Marley

The graveyard was overrun;
it was apparent loved ones
had stopped visiting
years ago

but it was peaceful—

a quietness
I experienced
nowhere else
permeated
the faded script
etched into headstones
and entrances to
cold marble mausoleums

abandoned bouquets
of assorted flowers
and baby's breath
scattered over
the barely-there path,
but I could still
make it out
when the moonlight shone
just right through
the skeletal trees

Xtina Marie

I sit near a cross,
and trace the name
deeply engraved
into the stone

Marlene Martin
Loving daughter, wife, mother

and a sadness stirs
within me

because I am
a loving daughter, wife, mother

I finger the dainty
gold necklace
with *Marley* inscribed into it
hanging from my neck
and I cry for this stranger
buried 6 feet beneath
where I sit

it's so quiet here

Compromise

He needed
a little
danger
in the
bedroom

and I needed
a little
safety…

we compromised
when he
whispered
sweet nothings
in my ear

as he lit
my ass up
with his hand

Alive

kiss me
like you hate me,
let me feel
your teeth scrape
across the delicate flesh
of my neck
while you
fist my hair
between your fingers
and yank
until I see stars,
whisper all
of the
filthy things
you want to do
to me
as you twist my arms
up and over
my head
so that I'm
painfully dancing
on my toes,
love me like you
hate me
when the tears
slide soundlessly

onto the pillow
and my throat is sore
from screaming
because we both know
I need a little pain
before I fully
feel alive

My Demons

the demons
I write about
are only the ones
I've befriended…

the ones
I recognize,
who call me
by name

ones I've been
acquainted with
for years and years

but there are others

others that haunt
not only
my dreams
but also
my waking hours
as well

the flitter about,
in shadows
here and there

always here
   always there

and they taunt me
with whispers
I pretend
not to hear

you're not good enough
you've never been good enough
you deserve all of the awful things
if they only knew the ugliness inside you

my greatest fear
is that

they might be right

Oddly Eternal

Not every
love story
has a
happily ever after

no sparkly fairytales
or magical sunset walk-offs
as we gaze
lovingly into
each other's eyes

some end in
broken glass
and blood staining
cold tile floors
that may in time fade,
unlike the internal scars
that are… oddly eternal

and

harsh words screamed
in fury,
shattering spirits
that are
much more difficult

to heal
than the bruises
placed carefully
under a light sweater

some love stories
begin as adorable
meet cutes
and accidental
insta loves,
the kind
neighbors and family
talk about as
serendipitous
or meant to be

while ending in
a white knuckled
psychological thriller

ours ended
with the panicked
sounds of screaming,
guttural and animalistic
as I fought for
my sanity
among the empty
liquor bottles
and fragments
of my mind

Xtina Marie

somewhere buried in
the debris
of an extreme horror novel

our love story
ended
with a bang,
and pain,
the harsh smeared maroon
seeping into
cracks in the floor…
> *oddly eternal*

Widowmaker

She was hiding
in the shadows…
her cruel,
blood-red lips
twisted in
a gruesome smile,
as she beckoned
him closer,
her sweet sensual
lullaby
cradling him
as he slipped
into her black
nothingness

panicking
I clawed at him,
screaming
his name
over and over
and over
trying to
release him
from her
clutches

while choking
on the stench
of death
permeating
from her pores

I wake
in a sweat,
the beeps from the
hospital equipment
surround me
as she fades
back into
the shadows,
whispers dying
on those
blood red lips:

I'm the Widowmaker, I'll be here
waiting for you...

Tuesday

Tuesday
9 miles one way
parking in the employee lot
I'll never find my car later
sandpaper tongue
legs asleep from sitting so long
I think the guy over there is homeless
waiting
hours pass
lady on the hospital phone *still*
too scared to cry
when do I call his mom? do I wait?
finally something, some news
directions to the ICU
could be directions to Syria for all I know
more waiting
doctor with the kind, gentle eyes
heart attack heart attack heart attack
paddles, blockage, stent, aFib
12%, 25%, very lucky
cold ICU room
awake, but disoriented
would she stfu about her damn ice cream
insides shaking
adrenaline falling
stomach pains

am I hungry? what time is it? when did I eat last?
bruised hands
beeping machines
I should have worn a different shirt
leaning over cold rails to kiss goodbye
nighttime
asking hospital security for help
relief to see the red convertible
dear Lord, please let me get home okay
walking up to the darkened house
dogs barking, Rosie screeching
cleaning up the mess
leftovers in the fridge
FRIENDS on the tv
exhausted but not tired
cold sheets
alone

A Little Lost

I'm a little
lost
right now,
not myself…
sometimes
I stare in the mirror
and a stranger
stares back
at me,
silently
judging me…
my skin
doesn't quite
fit me,
and I scratch
at the foreign feel
until I'm red
and rashed

maybe
this is a different me,
a new me…
someone born
from the embers
of the smoldering mess
the old me

Xtina Marie

left behind…

maybe this is
a better me
an older, wiser me,
a me who will
be called
Ma'am
instead of Miss,

whoever this
new me is,
I promise to
try and love her,
because I was
never too kind
to the old me

About the Author

The Short Version:
Book Publisher, Poet, Podcaster, Writer, Mom, Bibliophile…

The Accidental Poet:

Xtina Marie is an avid horror and fiction genre reader, who became a blogger; who became a published poet; who became an editor; who now is a book publisher and CEO of HellBound Books Publishing with her co-host on The Panic Room Radio Show, James H. Longmore.

Her first book of poetry, Dark Musings has received outstanding reviews. It is likely Xtina was born to this calling. Writing elaborate twisted tales to entertain her classmates in middle school would later lead Xtina to use her poetry as a private emotional outlet in adult life—words she was hesitant to share publicly—but the more she shared, the more accolades her writing received.

She is now an Amazon Best-Selling Poet and has written 9 other poetry books.

Xtina has contributed works to the following:
Suite 269 by Christine Zolendz
Busted Lip: An Anthology
Monsters of Metal: An Anthology
The Intermission, Gore Carnival Book 2
A Lovely Darkness: Poetry with Heart
Black Candy: A Halloween Anthology of Horror
Collected Christmas Horror Shorts by Kevin J. Kennedy
Slashing Through the Snow: A Christmas Horror Anthology
Depraved Desires: Volume 1
Beautiful Tragedies
Damsels of Distress
Pieces of Us: A Collection of Flash Fiction, Short Stories, and Poetry
Subliminal Messages: A Collection of Poetry, Prose, and Quotes
Leaves of the Poet Tree by Andrew Aitken
Apocalypse of the Heart by Leah Negron and friends
Poetry Friends in Rhythm & Rhyme by Leah Negron
Graveyard Girls by Gerri R. Gray
Further Within Darkness & Light: A Collection of Poetry by Paul B Morris
The Light Shines Through: Anthology of Poetry
Paper Cuts

The Horror Zine Magazine Summer 2024

Other titles by Xtina:
Light Musings
Darkest Sunlight
Without the Confines of My Rhymes
Immortalize Me
Wild, Imperfect & Messy
Where the Dirt Road Leads
From the Passenger Window
Greatest Hits

Xtina resides in the beautiful state of Tennessee, with her family, three yappy ankle biters and 2 ball pythons.

You can find Xtina:
http://www.hellboundbookspublishing.com/index.html
https://www.facebook.com/XtinaMarie4031/
https://www.facebook.com/ThePanicRoomRadioShow/
https://www.amazon.com/Xtina-Marie/e/B01E1QNI3O?ref=sr_ntt_srch_lnk_1&qid=1589142288&sr=8-1

OTHER POETRY FROM Xtina Marie
www.hellboundbookspublishing.com

Xtina Marie's Greatest Hits

"Ever wanted to know what a person's soul looks like? In this vulnerable, eclectic book of poetry, the writer flays open her soul and bleeds onto each page, giving her readers a rare glimpse into the essence of who she is. Raw, beautiful, and poignant!"

- *K Webster*, USA Today Bestselling Author

"Dark and delightful poet Xtina Marie has such a beautiful way with words—I'm a fan already, but 'Xtina's Greatest Hits' has me obsessed! I wanna make Xtina Marie wall collages and fill 100 notebooks in tiny black-print handwriting! Just kidding… mostly. (In all seriousness, read this book! It's dreamy.)"
--*Staci Layne Wilson*, author of the 'Rock & Roll Nightmares' book series

From the Passenger Window

"Xtina Marie doesn't just have a way with words, she commands them." - Samantha Downing, USA Today bestselling author.

"From the Passenger Window is a stunning collection of poetry that is a breathtaking journey through the joys and sorrows of life, expertly crafted with vivid imagery and emotional depth.

Xtina Marie's words have the power to transport you to the crisp, sun-kissed days of summer and evoke the heady rush of new love, while also honoring the heart-wrenching pain that shapes us into who we are.

From the Passenger Window is a must-read for anyone who loves to get lost in the beauty of language and explore the raw, complex emotions that make us human."
-Debra Anastasia, USA TODAY Bestselling Author

Where the Dirt Road Leads

"I fell in love with this poetry from Xtina, rereading certain passages (like You've Always Been). There is a depth to the emotion that lingers and, to me, that's what makes poetry what it is." - USA Today, Wall Street Journal and #1 Contemporary Bestselling Romance Author Willow Winters

"Xtina cuts along the edges of love and loss with a hopeful precision that feels sublime for the pain." - M Ennenbach

The Dark Poet Princess is back with her newest book of beautifully crafted free verse poetry. Where the Dirt Road Leads takes us on a journey as Xtina celebrates life and love in a way that's so very relatable and raw. We relive past demons she's still fighting and we mourn with her as she cries. A new adventure awaits at every turn of the page, and she welcomes you to take her hand and follow her where the dirt road leads.

Wild, Imperfect & Messy

Xtina Marie is easily a poet who deserves more readers. Her latest collection takes us through a journey of sharp moments. Each poem makes an incision, slowly peeling back layers of beautiful darkness, heartache, and experiences that will dig deep into readers' hearts. The verses within offer a glimpse into memories and hopes, and into the raw chaos that makes us all human. "A collection that is not to be missed!" -Sara Tantlinger, Bram Stoker Award-winning author of The Devil's Dreamland

Immortalize Me

"Immortalize Me is raw, beautiful, and poignant. This subtle yet hypnotic dance between darkness and light is a poetry lover's delight!"

- USA Today Bestselling Author, K Webster

With a style echoing the late Audre Lorde, Xtina Marie's newest poetry collection Immortalize Me - with its striking imagery and layered free-verse simplicity - reveals a provocative, candid look at Xtina's story told in fragments - intimate snapshots of moments of submission and raw passion, nostalgia and drifting daydreams, anguish and quiet contemplation. All in all, a bold, haunting, bittersweet collection.

"As lyrical as song and as faceted as a diamond, Xtina Marie's latest collection is a riot of imagery and emotion that pushes buttons and boundaries alike. IMMORTALIZE ME does just what it says - her words will linger in your blood long after the last page has been read."

- Alistair Cross, author of The Book of Strange Persuasions and the Vampires of Crimson Cove series

Without the Confines of my Rhymes

Poetry is a beautiful thing, illustrating thoughts and emotions with concise, well-chosen words. A lot of poetry rhymes, adding additional flavor to the words, giving them a sense of rhythm, of flow

But what happens when you take away the rhyming, when you cast off the forms of convention and good sense?

Then the interesting things begin to come out. When the next line doesn't need to rhyme, anything can come next. As it is within the poems themselves, so it is with this book in its entirety.

Casting off the rhyming styles she used before, Xtina Marie embarks on a journey of emotional ups and downs, reflecting on love, loss, children and art.

So settle in, put on your wine-colored glasses, and take a trip without the confines of rhymes.

Darkest Sunlight

"The heart was made to be broken."
- *Oscar Wilde*

To allow your heart to soar, you must risk the depths. Darkest Sunlight is the third poetic narrative from Xtina Marie. In this journey, readers will begin in the darkest of places yet revealed to us by this critically acclaimed poet, only to then find themselves thrust into the brightness of love before their eyes and minds can fully adjust.

It is this shocking contrast which best conveys what it is to love, lose, and love again.

In Dark Musings, Xtina explored sadness. In Light Musings, she explored the intricacies of a loving heart. In Darkest Sunlight, Xtina Marie compares the opposite ends of the spectrum, and in doing so, she found a place darker than black.

Light Musings

What a web she weaves. Light Musings is a poetic narrative—a story told through related poems. Xtina Marie is a master of this style. Known by her fans as the Dark Poet Princess. This term of endearment came about as a result of the horror genre embracing her first book: Dark Musings which continues to garner stellar reviews.

Light Musings will not disappoint her loyal fans as darkness is present within these pages as well. However, this latest book will show a much larger audience that Xtina's poetry pulls out every feeling the reader has ever experienced—forcing them to feel with her protagonist. Light Musings shows us that love is made from darkness and light; something Xtina Marie explores like no one else.

Dark Musings

"Poetry that jumps off the page and squeezes your heart. I loved every word." -New York Times bestselling author, Alessandra Torre. The dark side of Xtina Marie's poetry delves into intense emotions: heartache, loss, hurt, pain, rage, and a dangerous consuming love which can drive one insane. Dark Musings is not a collection! The author returned to the centuries old practice of Narrative Poetry—the telling of a story through poetry. If you believe you are brave enough to explore the savage emotions of the human heart; Dark Musings will test your mettle.

"Poetry the jumps off the page and squeezes your heart. I loved every word." -New York Times bestselling author, Alessandra Torre.

A HellBound Books Publishing LLC Publication

http://www.hellboundbooks.com/

Printed in the United States of America